Contents

AFTER WORDS

AFTER WORK

Introduction

Here is a man who knows the world's of work and love and the natural creation through the simple expedient of going about in those worlds. These are poems from the world about us, not literary poems, not willed poems, you might call them response poems--in the sense that, for all the gentle introspection, what moves Jim Brennan to the poem is otherness, the sense that ours is a populated multiverse, where other beings have their lives as deeply and compellingly as we have ours, as the poet has his.

These are journeyman poems of testament and testing: he tells us what he sees, moves in the poems through what he sees to what he knows; they are testing poems in the sense not only that he is testing the world against some instinct of what is true register, but also in the sense that the poems test us, like creatures moving out across unsure ground. You have the sense here that what the poems will risk as disclosure depends on our willingness to have their mysteries disclosed. Our willingness to read with open heart, open mind.

When Brennan writes

"I was him once, I did what he does"

there is self-knowledge there, and knowledge of the other; the perception requires the reader's self-knowledge to complete the circuit.

When he writes

"Bring your thoughts
Outside yourself
Come inside of me
Leave your hand on me
Leave your weight".

the invitation is not just to the loved one, it is also to the unknown but knowable reader.

These are poems of trust in human community, poems of respect and love and understanding, forms of conversation with the living and the dead, the friend, lover and neighbour as well as the stranger not yet met, the reader over his shoulder. Trust is perhaps the ultimate naïve gesture, and yet, if there is a common thread running through these poems it is a thread of trust. Does this mean the poems are naïve? Sometimes, often, yes. There are poems here that are awkward in their naivety, over-hesitant in their questioning, reticent where another poet might have forced the conclusion--and very likely missed the point. Brennan's world is one where only the quiet certainties may be trusted, everything else is unsure:

> "How it amplifies itself
> May leave you breathless"

he says, knowing that to be breathless is also to be without words, without the power to speak. And yet, time and again he finds the power to speak, to search out ways of naming grace:

> "Sometimes in the quietness
> Of myself I speak".

These are gentle poems, poems of quiet aspiration towards the human. The poet mourns his dead, salutes his friends, looks carefully and with respect on strangers casually encountered. He looks at and listens to himself as a creature no different to them, neither better nor worse, and he speaks to us in his own voice, hesitant but unafraid:

> "Sometimes we find
> In the soft lilt
> Of an accent a quiet wisdom"

Quiet wisdom. Exactly.

Theo Dorgan

This book is dedicated to the memory
of
Freda Rountree
and
Michael Hartnett

Acknowledgements

Acknowledgements are due to the following:

The Editors of Tullamore Tribune, Co. Offaly and Midland Tribune, Birr. Also to Midlands Radio; 3FM Tullamore, where some of the poems were first published or broadcast.

My thanks to Laurence Boland, Phibsboro, Dublin, for the use of his photographs in this publication.

Photographs on pages............... © Terence Smeaton

After Love

Red and White in the Mist

For Olwyn and Jeff

In a season of mist
They say I was born
My father proud and tall in his walk
Is torn with pride
He looks out over Ballaghmore
To the white fog on the morning grass.
The sun is rising in its usual way
From the east
Across the sea over the edge
Casting its rays all over me
A child called Olwyn
The light of the morning
In my baby eyes
Calls me to my
New Castle.

But all of this is in the future
Somewhere upriver
Behind my shoulder
On a country farm in England
My future love awaits me
In his little rubber boots
Climbing through the hay and the bushes
Disturbing the early flight
Of morning thrushes
He is in search of warm brown eggs
Then
The sunlight through the red and white
Falls down from the clouds
Of a small Irish town
Where my thoughts are forming.

And where some day
A poet with blue eyes
Will come
To bless us with words
Out perhaps
Of the mist
Of where I was born.

Leaves in Autumn
For Roy and Mary

There is a purr of an engine
Behind your ear
Everything is high octane
A blur through the light
In the mid-day sun the sliotar
Is lost in space
The heart misses a beat
In the heat and passion of play
A blessing through the
Falling leaves of AUTUMN
Found us close together
Caressed into one another
Into the winds of time
But this is not a rhyme as such
It is just to say
I love you very much
There is nothing else to say
Except to know the day we met
Was high octane
A sliotar in space
And the words you sometimes
Whisper behind my ear
Light as leaves falling
In the autumn time
Of the year.

The Dancer

For Jimmy and Mary

I don't even want to leave here,
This little glimpse of heaven.
I have met the angels here
They carve words out
Of the still air.
They shape the dark ink
Across the page
They conjure up the image
Of the new.
Like the elegance of a dancer's feet
That triptapping sound.
And like the dancers
They hold gently each other.
Their words float
Down through the bright day
Like cherry blossoms
Gliding into the Feale.
Words and shapes
Sounds floating out into
The broad world of the sea.

A Walnut Moon
For Liz

I keep thinking about the night
The moon married us across the
Walnut trees
Did you see me in my working boots
Proud to be alive
Not knowing the difference between planets
Or what orbited what
We had clay at our heels
And I can never put into words
The way the light caught the stone
Gable of your face
Or the weave of your hair
I was as frightened as you
And what I feel for you right now
Or at any other time
Will be like the moon
Pulling itself up
Over our eternal
Childlike heads.

Blackberries
For Jerri

She has blackberry eyes
Dark and slender
The sun catches the bones of her face
I imagine all kinds of things
About her
I ate the petals of the flowers
Thinking I could taste her
Sonidos negros
Are words I cannot write to her,
But she is so curiously beautiful.
What pain is she hiding
Behind her dark eyes.
The mountains are full of sounds
And water too lies in deep places
Her face and manner is elegant
She walks always out of the sea
Her life has drawn her to exotic islands
She is following her road to heaven
The mountains are falling down
Into her
I want to drink her in and taste
Her salty tongue.

Hill of the Sheep - Cappinageeragh
For Mark and Noreen

Sleeping with you in my dreams
Dreaming of you in my sleep
Waking on my own again
Were you ever here at all
Was it you calling me
Or me reaching out to you
I could feel you breathing me in.
Blowing to me near my listening ear.
Last night was a whole year long
Without you.
Dreaming in my sleep
A shepherd after sheep
The lost lamb
Resting on my shoulder
My crook and staff protects you
Sleeping with you
In my dreaming
Over the hills dreaming into sleep
The sheep are quiet
Among the hills of sleep
Their shepherd watches
The mantle of his thoughts are sure to keep
The dreamers dreaming into sleep
Then I am reaching out to you
Breathe me in
We will hurt no more.

Red Haired Golden
For Yvonne and Filly

I was lost on the dark road to Golden
Looking for a girl
With fire in her hair
She was there
Somewhere in the dark
Her voice somewhere in the recent air
I could see the spark of her walking
Soon I wished
Wishing to be talking with my
Flamed haired girl
Caressing her with speech
And sleepless too
In the long dark of her golden
Lost in the heat and light of
One another
I will play slow airs
And elegant tunes to her
The bow of my fiddle
Dancing up and down
In and out of reels
We'll go together
To the golden
In the dark
The fire of her hair
Lighting up the night.

A Cloth to keep

For Kate & Joan
Kilcar Workshop Summer Palace

Turn me over you
Allow yourself to touch
Weave me into you
Put your colours
Into every thread
Fold me into you
Bring me with you
In your pocket
Bring your thoughts
Outside yourself
Come inside of me
Leave your hand on me
Leave your weight
To me
Share your breath your mouth
Your tongue
Your eyes
And what you see in me
Crumple up the threads
You have of me
The cold and heat of me
Safe just at your fingers keep
A cloth at times
To weep sometimes
To weave me into you.

In case we go walking

The day came at last
When we walked
But I could not speak
I was taking you in
You were quiet also
You allowed me this quiet
Privilege
I pillaged you with
My thoughts
When I was behind you.
Then you turned and
Looked into me
There were no words
Speech was beyond us
Lost in the water lap
Of one another
But as none of this
Has happened yet
As it is still
Up river somewhere
Behind my shoulder
I fall back into
The present tense
And let my wishing
Drift skywards
Into the air.

The Oars in the Air

For Cara Cunningham

The oars rise up
Dripping back into the sea
The sea swells up its salt belly
The wind whips through your hair
The cliffs move over slow move
Dancing in the air
The land is far away from us
Shoals of fish follow
The gulls are hunting well today
Wide their wings against the blue light
Our oars again rise up
The sinews in my arms are pounding
My back bending to and fro
My thighs grow stronger
I drive my feet against the floor
I force the whole power of myself
Into the soft wetness
I twist and spin
I am at the beginning
My neck I make into an arch
Down my spine my cords loosen
The oars rise up, then plunge deep in
Rise up deep in,
You keep to grip
I turn my hip into the wild of the wind
My hands let go my fingers stiff
Like fish the foam spurts
The tail flicks the gills flesh out
The boat rises one last time
We float back somewhere into shore

The oars lie quietly side by side.

Wine from the vine...
For Joyce, Mike, Hannah and Barry

Joyce with the wonderful smile
Your voice booming out across the room
In the laughter of your face
Your daughter turned me into high disgrace.

All over trees we went
Children throwing colours into the high
Of each others imagination.

There will be wine from the vine of life
To celebrate beginnings
And we will dream of redwood trees
Reaching for the light.

We will laugh in each others company
Hannah with paint beneath her nails.
Mick a triangular man in the making
String cheese between your teeth.

Let us forever keep each other in the palm
of our hands
Living and laughing into the high lands.

The soft fields
For Ali

When first I observed her
The golden silence of her
Like a field of wheat she was
Waving in the wind because
All over her the coat she wore
Reminded me of things I'd seen
Slowly dressing down to skin
The landscape of her breasts I saw
The mountains of her thighs between
Her breathing and her sighs and then;
Her hair as soft as eiderdown
Below her eyes the twinkle there,
The fields of flesh
The greening there
Her rivers floating everywhere
The softness of the dew in her
That trickles slowly into heat
My breathing in the early air
My fingers moist into her touch.
The morning birds drift up and out
A slow dance high
And songs as such
As come between
Her far and near distance.
I am far below her now
Turning in my sleep I see
The colour of her hair behind
A tree still standing where I stood
Observing her; the golden in the quiet of
her
The landscape hidden in the coat she wore.

The light at your shoulder

I could stay forever
Beneath the Roscrea
Moon of Saturday
Waiting for the sun
To rise above
Your shoulder
You would be
Caught in its early
Arrival
But in between
The now and then
It's just survival
For who ever
Can laugh the most
With the moon
Like a host
In the sky.

Helen Rising

Helen is rising up to me
Out of the kitchen
Forever busy
Her smile can make
The knees grow weak
And if I could speak the words
To her
That I really mean to say
She would not be ready to
Believe me.
So I am consigned to the
Lonely table near the window
Myself my pen; my cigarettes
The red wine from Chile
Warming to my bones
The stone of her standing
The strength of her waiting
In the rivers of wine
She is running again
Away with three rings
In her ear,
Perhaps a year to our mating
Or is Helen dating
Helen again is rising to me
Out of her busy kitchen.

For Sean. T. and Rosie
a wedding blessing

He got lost in her
long smile
And she in his.

Losing themselves
In each others arms
Folding into
And reaching into
Holding hands across
The bridge of caring.
And this is young love
Crossing the canal
At Molesworth house - to one another
In this caressing
In this kissing.

May this two make one
And then this three together
Make another
And may the father love the mother
Even more
And may this four go on forever
In the memory of us all
And in this love
may the holy dove that moves in them
Make five
And may this family
Be alive to life.
Let us bless them
Calling children running in the wind

Of what we call tomorrow
And may their sorrows
If they have any;
Fall away like shadows
And lose each other
All together
In their long smiles.

Explaining myself
for Kevin "The Deputy" Dunne

You may allow yourself to imagine
Me naked
Under the broad sky
You do not need to reason this out
Or to apply any rules
Moral or otherwise
Because you are human
With fears and emotions
That are almost always
Just at the surface behind your eyes
We angels realise this
In mortal people
We are constantly
Trying to be like you
And to carry you always
Under our invisible wings.

The Lovers and the flood
after the painting by Michael Scott
For Annie

Safely we sleep
After our journey with the fish
They rest in our opposite direction
My cheek is numb
Against the stubble of your face.

Caressed without reason
In our season of grace
When you move you are as gentle
As the ripple of fish.
Dreaming themselves
From the blue, back home
Upstream into the river.

The gold of my sleeves cuff
Against the stripe
Of your waistcoat
Your tear is salt
To my tongue.

Hold me beyond words
Lull me soon
Out of the sensual light
Let the moon pull us into
The new blue
Of the morning.

High Arrival
For my granddaughter Abbie

In the heat of lust we arrive;
From the dust of days
We fall into the ways of love.
But we must rise above
The words of men
Into the deep of the sea.
To the quiet and the dark
Above our heads.
Instead of light
We are at the beginning.
To the murmur of speech
To the talk of people.
Into the air
And in the steeple of stone
We must allow ourselves to soar.
We walk away from each other
Trying for the light.
And in our eyes recall
That all is forever frozen
In the thrust of days.
And from the swirl and turn of dust
All men are made.
Around your feet and in each others arms
We meet;
Lost in a moment.
A new child
In the high and lust

Of just arriving.

Lost in the River

I was turning the corner into tomorrow
Thinking of words or
How I might say them
I spend all my life saying goodbye
With words sometimes trapped
In the back of my throat
There I am walking down
Near that place by the river
With sounds tumbling in to the lap
Of the water
Perhaps something soft
In the way of her speech
Or the words of her thoughts
In the things she might say
With all of our coming
And all of our going
I wait for the listening
Of her going away.
Without the words
That I meant her to hear
Sounds that are gone
Away with tomorrow
Turning the corner
Lost
Somewhere up river.

For Sarika

There is fog among the trees
Out in the wood
And courage in the songs of early birds
There is a girl I wish to know
In my dreaming she is sometimes
Where the bluebells grow.
With the sweet smell of apples
In her hair
I have sometimes thought of her,
The secret space of her
And dreamed my fingers touching
Her soft;
Her skin.
Or my words mixing sounds with hers
She is Afrikaner with her thoughts
Sarika sprinkled
On her native place
Like paprika dust.
Someday she knows she will return;
To her farm home, until then
She is bound to time
And will make time to roam among the
green Island
Swelling up and out
Of the Atlantic
She has not heard yet the lonesome
Cry of the curlew
Or the manly song of the corncrake
For my sake I hope she stays forever
So I can let her hear the wild roar of the sea
Or walk with her among the
High trees in the wood.

The Busy Street

Before I had even met her
My thoughts had violated her
But
I put this down to being a man
Whatever that is.
I did not speak about her to anyone
I saw her
Everyday on the streets out walking
She passed by without a look.

There I am talking in my sleep sometimes
Where I see glimpses of her
The silence of her
Wishing for the presence of her speech
At last then; we are sitting near
She gives my voice a listening ear
A day a week a month a year since
We are on our own
Sometimes among the crowded streets
In all the faces that we meet
There is someone there
Who has never met
Some girl he sees out walking
Quietly towards him
Lonely there inside himself.

Hopi Prophesy

When the earth is ravaged and the animals
are dying
A new tribe of people shall come unto the
earth
From many colours, classes and creeds.
And who by their actions and deeds.
Shall make the earth
Green again as warriors of the rainbow.

Hopi Virgin Child

She has long and tangled me her hair
She is like the Hopi virgin
Still a child
Here with the morning shadows on her face.
Like early flowers across a field
Or the silhouette of trees
Before my eyes.
In the soft half light
Here in the quiet when the night lifts
And the sometimes pink of the new day
comes.
When I can see the rhythms
In the bones of her face
And watch her in the quiet.
Where the wind is still.
Everytime I see her face
She fills my day with lost thoughts
When she tangles me her hair
Sweet smell of apples hidden there.
My Hopi girl
My little rainbow child.

Inside Yourself
for Martin Pius Kelly

It was a room full of people
But each one was
Allowed to be themselves

People did not congregate here
In groups to stare you down

Where there is that liberation
Of being allowed to come
And become part of yourself
No one will question
Who you are
Each is equal before each other
You are not who you seem to be
You transform into a form that is neither

Who you were
Or anyone you imagine yourself to be
You get lost into the mind
Becoming one body
        One spirit
        In Christ

WE are you we are you
You are we you are we

High flyer
for Sarah

She's a woman
Who can make me high
With laughter
Her thigh invites you in
She can bend herself
Around her brush
A high heel queen
A thrush
As tasty I bet
As asparagus tips
And the hips
O the hips of her
The high elegance
Of her walking away
Has me wishing
She would stay longer
The bounce of her eye
As she tosses her hair
Back in the air at the shoulder
There's none so brave
And bolder as my London
Irish lass
A lady of class
With high silk to her collar
I will make bread for
Her someday on my
Ould melodian

Liena

Liena that I see
Sometimes on the street
Although time will pass
And we may never meet
I think perhaps sometimes
The moon over Latvia
Is lonely for you.
Hiding its loneliness behind a high cloud
Lost in the loud crying of your leaving.
You are far away in La Serenta
Going headlong into the future.
The flow of your red hair
Dancing through the slow air
At your shoulder.
Red as the high red
Of the setting sun
You have only just begun
Your journey towards the west.
May you forever have the best of good
company,
And let the smile on your face
Light up the blue eyes of your lover.
Lienna that I sometimes see
Walking on the street
Time is passing and we may never meet.

My Wonderful People
The Clashroe Poem

I have invented black people for you
The yellow and the brown people
Far away in the frozen air in their warm
igloo
I have given the image of my children
Dying to you.
Across time and space
The human race I made for you
Hymen the god of love
I gave to you.
The language in their mouths
The tongue twisting
Sounds around your ears
But you do not hear me
Teaching you every day
The words you need to say
How you must respect each other
With the look of love
Peace I give you
Forever within the grasp of doves
Floating towards me in the sky
This is why my children die
Because you do not listen
I am calling you
My dark my coloured
My wonderful people.
I am calling you.

To a woman

Floating on the frantic edge of myself
Singing the shape the colour
And the aroma that you make
The fantastic-ness of you
The fear of falling fills my days
I am trying to find the words
The way to say the thoughts of love
To hold me, caress me in your thinking
Catch me floating,
Smiling but frantic on the edge of things.
All ahead is unpredictable
The very next moment
Already gone.
We must celebrate each others company
Free each other of suspicion and fear
Try to be aware of how time
Turns out waking hours into years.
Try like men
To let the tears we want to cry
Loose and out into the light of days.
And to understand the ways of women
they who are curious in shape
Attractive in their form
Pleasing to the eye.
To realise that a day will come
When each one of us will die
And become a story
In some gathering
Frantic on the edge of things.

On Drinking Marion's Auburn Wine

In whitewalls near the lap of the water
By degrees and honours
My mind was made--
Wine from the vine
Fruit from the rolling
Roads of Tyrone
O the bouquet of it
The elegance of its colour
As auburn as its creator--
A Burndennet special
Vintage year.
As the falcon
Swoops down through
The air
Death in its claws
Towards the beating heart
The last sound lost
In the lap of water
Near Whitewalls.

Annie: In the high blue

I could not tell her; of my dreams
In all I do or say
I could not tell her of the way it was
The sun made night time thinking, wake me
into day
Our tumbling and our rolling out
Her breathing soft throughout my hair
Her whispering into my ear
Her words are still clear
As water spinning into flood
Our flowing down into each other
As only lovers should
Her legs her arms
Her holding close
Her trembling thighs
Her calling out
Her back she arches
To the light
The stillness of her sleeping then
Her breathing warm down near my breast
Her navel moving up and down
Her crumpled clothes
Her dressing gown
My fingers walking up and down to that
place where men forget
Their beginning and begetting
But I must lie here all alone
As cold as ice as still as stone
And never tell her of my dreaming
Our coming
Into the early air

Our going into mists
The nothingness of mist
In mist
The white clouds
Loud across the sky
But I cannot forget her sighs
'across the high blue'
I cannot tell her of my dreams of her.

After Thoughts

Dreamtime 1

Even your dreams
Can kill you
You wake in the darkness
Of yourself
To find it's only you
Beside yourself, inside the
Thoughts that would explain
You
The light changes everything
The eye seeks explanation
The ear finds sounds
That are only words
Forming.
The feet and hands are
Grasping for the familiar.
But that's what dreaming
Can sometimes be

We are sleeping back
Inside ourselves – where
All you can do is go
Where the dreaming
Brings you
Even if somewhere
In the darkness
You can see yourself
Climbing over the hills
Of sleep
The bells
And the light
Will change everything

It's only 3am
You awake on the
Wrong side of the coin
Your eye explaining
Your ear listening
Your feet and hands
Grasping for the familiar
Because even your dreams
Can kill you.

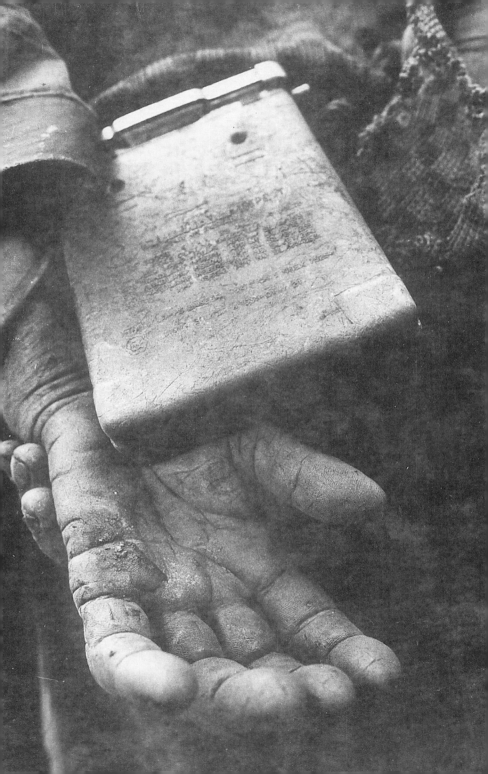

Into your hands

Every day the geometry of what you do
Has to come back to vertical
The shape of the space between
Your hands
Forever brings you back to a starting point
For we must never forget the history of
things
The building of houses
The caressing of people

The maker of dreams
The longing to forget
How time brings distances
To remembering
How the present comes to be
How the wind might caress a stone
How the moss softens out.

In the rains we came
From the turning of clay we are made
But this is lost to our memory
A place where the heart longs for
But our feet cannot carry us to
We are frozen in the imaginary light
Not in our sight;
Just below the surface in our senses.
Waiting for the wind to bring us back
To vertical
Into the shape between our hands.

In reply to Mr Yeats 1994

I have found the embroidered cloths
Of heaven that you speak of,
Laid out in the west they are
With stone through hills and fields
See out there for all to see
This woven cloth of green
Made from threads of blue and yellow
At buttercup time of year
Here the dreams are walked upon
And worked with strong and tired hands
Down through time this needlework
Sewn out in the green soft lands.

About Jim

Far beyond the place
We call ourselves
Somewhere far away
From home
I have a high elegant
Feeling like a lost soul.
But there is a prayer
Left in you - still there
And it starts to remember
You.
Save me from myself
It says.
Save me from myself
It prays.
The light is pulling
Itself around you.
Like a mantle
To the flame.
There is a flicker of
Recognition
You begin to call
A name
You are calling
In the voice of days.
Your small feet
Touch the ground.
In this calling
In this place
You do not hear the
Sound
Floating far above
Yourself.

You try to hide from
Pain
The nets you tangled
To my feet
The wounds you leave
Behind
Like a half moon
In the morning
Sleeping in the high blue.
I don't know
What I did
To you.

The Vanishing

He looked like one of
Those peculiar people
Like he was finished;
His work by mid morning
It was the way
He looked
At the traffic
And lit his cigarette
At the same time.

When I looked up
From writing
He had disappeared
Vanished into the air
Of my memory.

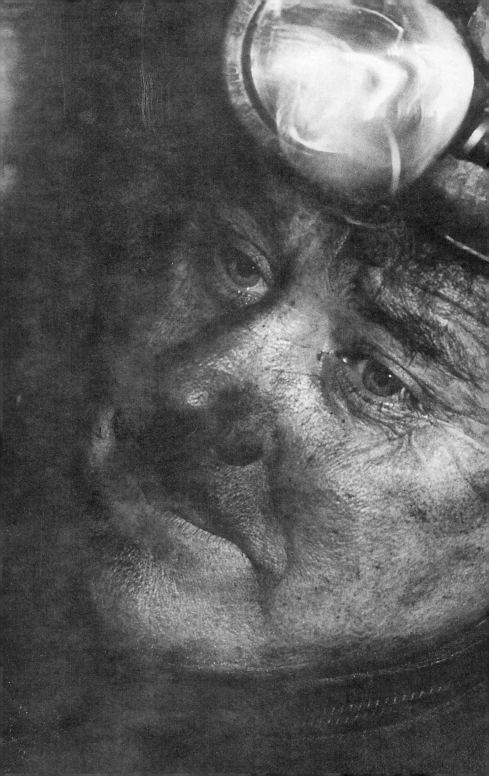

Middle Age

So here I am
With a slight ache in the arms
That I somehow know
Someone someday
Will do their best
To comfort
Or allow me look out some window
At the setting west
The sun as red as I remember it
Across the callows and the places
Long gone into memory
But for now it is just a slight
Ache in the arms
Looking at the past
Is all that is clear to me
Forever in my eyes in front of me
Driving into the future
Just behind me at my shoulder
Out in front of me the past.

For Markus

Termon House, Donegal

How the landscape decides
What it will allow us to see
In its own distress
Bulging up through grass
The numbers turn into language
Not an all knowing language
Words decide their own importance.
Like something unfamiliar
Beckons the eye
Reserves for itself what it will allow
The heart to see
Where history has no reason to ever exist
For we must allow
Whatever space that is our allocation
The time to educate us;
To forever teach us its mystery
In the end it is the landscape
That decides our fate.

Noble and Calm
for Annie A.

Annie with the fire
In her tail.
That smoke lingering
At the back of her eyes
Reluctant to speak at first
But a thirst for conversation
All the same
I barely know her name
But still she has words to say;
I can see her
Someday through a candle
On a table
Bread fresh from the oven
Some neat native American
Dish and even sambuca
Fire licking itself
Into the air
It might be summer
Across Rathmines
With all the worlds
A world away
But if we needed to
We could run to the lights
Of the city
Or cast our lines and thoughts astray
Me with my grey beard
And her with fire
In her tail.

Sometimes Snow

Snow wherever it falls
Has the peculiar shape
Of angels.

With faces
That fold into each other.
Falling forward into time
Suddenly I find myself
Walking over a silent place.
Sometimes in the quietness
Of myself I speak
Then going back
I gently step
Across the face of others
Going towards
That place I came from
Into the everywhere
Heat of the sun.

Confirmation Day
For Robbie Broderick

In our arms we held you
Your soft new blonde hair
We carried you all this way
Safe so far
To Confirmation Day
Now you can look to all sides
Strong at last
Making up your own mind
At where you might find
What God hides
For all the days that lie ahead
Now you have the power to see
The things that only
Sometimes can be seen
By looking back to what has been
When you were just a child
And feel again the arms
That held you
And bring you here all this way
To Confirmation Day.

Mass on Christmas Day

He was gentle in his awkward walk
Bent almost over
His wrists turned inward
His feet not altogether straight
I admired him; I envied his courage
To make his way like everybody else
All the way up to the top of the church.
Then it all started over again
On his way back down
One or two impatient people
Passed him
Muttering something underneath
Their cold breaths
Still smiling he soldiered on.
Was he marching in his head?
Proud to make it back to his seat
Gentle and strong at Christmas Mass
He brought the light into me
That morning
Like he was a little baby Jesus
In disguise.

I Me You
For Dermot and Helene

I am sometimes a leaf curious in the light
I am bending sometimes in the wind of you
I am lying alone with the sounds that stones
make.
I am staring up into the gallball light of the
moon.
You are me floating up into the sky.
Sweeping over the tall shape of the town.
I am the ring around my shoulder.
You are spinning in the heat of the light.
I am the soft wind behind your ear.

I am twisting the light.
You are the shadows outside yourself.

I am nothing other that what I dream myself
to be.
I am sometimes, somewhere in your
memory.
Sometimes I am lost to me.
I am sometimes here, I am forever there.

Peace M.S.J. Roscrea

You directed me down
To where the copper coloured
Stones were sleeping
Covered in the swift
Tra-lap and loop
Of the water
Tra-lap and loop
Through the rocks
Over mosses
Soothing all my fears
Carrying them away
Down into the past
Disappearing around
The next bend
The future is always near
And right behind
My shoulder.

Digging a hole to China

So there are five children
Digging a hole with plastic
Shovels
I say
What are you digging
A well or what?
No we're lookin' for lava
No we're not
We're diggin' a hole to China
Or else we might
Dig under the tree
And find fairies
I say
O yes that makes
Perfect sense.

On meeting a tourist

For Paddy and Mary Byrne, ESSO Daingean

Hello I said
He looked, made some
Strange
Sound that landed down
Along the ground where
I was kneeling
Working at a wall.

I looked at him so tall
Oh to be a tourist.
Give me a quare cap
A pink shirt
A pair of check trousers
And a funny underpants
So I can be a tourist.

Straying here and going there
Without a worry or a care
Let me go and stare at stones
Or examine ancient bones
Let me rest myself to dine
Give me peace and fine red wine.

But most of all my greatest thirst
Is to become a tourist
With soft white cap
Bright pink shirt
A pair of check trousers
(short ones)
And a funny underpants.

Dublin Airport Escalator

When the hours flew past us
She made him smile
Then he made me smile

Although I have never
Met him or her.

He was eighty going on twenty one
At least that's what
He looked like
When she strolled by
In her tight jeans.

Little did she know
Or ever could;
That she had brought
Two new smiles
into the world.

Funny how some people
Can do good.
I suppose we all do
But we never get to
Know about it.

After Words

Sins in my pocket

Perhaps that's
The way Angels
Are
They come back to
Us
In the shape
That we remember
Them by

For the sins I commit
I am a poet
It's a hard
Way to get to heaven

I can't even remember
A day without poems

For seven days
A week I am a poet

I must have an awful
Lot of sins
In my pockets.

Crucifixion - M.S.J. Roscrea

Here's to Bro Peter's corner
Of the world
With broken pieces
Old thrown out clothes
Cardboard faces
He praises God.
And turns over to us
The things that we find hard
To understand
His right hand nailed
His left hand also
Both feet
With a fertiliser bag
His wrapping cloth
Here in Bro Peter's world
He is
Collecting everybody's
Lost dreams
And broken hearts.

After dinner clothes line

Somedays it's good just to sit
And watch the clothes dry
It's truly amazing what happens
In the distance beyond.
You might see blackbirds
Drifting after each other
The towels are furiously
Waving them away.
"Come on ye boys in green"
On your T-shirt
Is trying his best
To be seen
He's calling them in.
The socks are glad just to be resting
Remembering the shape of someone's feet
The clothes pegs know all this
And this is where they
Forever meet.
Today they held up a poem for me.

For a Belfast girl in Clare
For P.A. Moore

Because sound is such
A power source to us
Forever surrounds us
In our waking hours.
Of for that matter in the songs
Of our dreaming
How it amplifies itself
Can sometimes leave you breathless
A sound; as old as the sea
A child cry to alert our beginnings
The sometimes cruel sound of laughter
A necessary sin.
The sound you cannot hear
Like pure joy; in the eyes
The echo of the stones
Protesting to their coming home.
To a tightness of skin
To make a drum.
Someone's triumphant tymphanum
To another a fear in the bottom
Of the stomach.
Or the high sound of voices
In a Latin chant
From a cloistered cubicle.
All is sound
To warm and console
To warn and to consume
A necessary dying
Of a beast.

A falling through stalks
In a garden
All is a necessary sound of returning.

Sometimes we find
In the soft lilt
Of an accent a quiet wisdom
As gentle as a fall
Sideways into silence.

From out of the space
That rises out of our landscape I find
The hidden lost songs
Of us all.

A New Language   Termon House

How utterly barbarian
You made us speak
As for now
We must use that language
That holds no music for us;
It betrays that ancient trust
That was forever our inheritance.
We move about across your lawns
Skipping into some foreign dance.

But we have discovered
Moments silences
Where fears away;
We allow ourselves to fall
Sideways into ditches
Alone to the earth
Into a singing river,
We will flow into the future
A place in some others heart
Someone's voice will carry us
To our new beginning.

A meek people
Slowly inhabiting the earth
Uttering our own true language.

A constant healing
God may be everything to everyone

In all things there is a constant healing
A quietness in the growing
Trying to see the invisible; to name them
And to bring out into the light
A simple goodness; in this
There is a constant healing.
Even when your heart is breaking
There is a constant healing.
When all hope is gone
There is a constant healing.
And when all the healing's done
There is a constant healing.

Slieve Bloom

For Derek and Rosiland

I take a little water
From the stream of words
Full it cools my thirst
With its ancient wisdom
This water has come down
Through the ages
From the holy men
And pagan sages
I am left to translate
Left to contemplate
Between my fingers
The wisdom of a piece of moss
Turning the past
Into my own words
Trying to understand
The knowledge of the mountains.

The Fifth Elementis
For Mark

Time does not exist
Only life exists
Time _is_ only a vapour
Life is a solid thing
Time is not important enough
It is life that is precious.

Time stops and starts
Constantly beginning
Life is the real cycle of becoming
Moving our hearts
A going away from darkness
Into the light
As the light forms us to itself
We are perhaps the fifth element
Of all that is around us.

The power, Helious, Master, Yahweh
God of all things
Deep within ourselves
Waiting for the finding out;
The naming of things
Remembering that
Time does not exist
Only life
Constantly exists.

I see him

If I could only throw my thoughts
Out into the sea
And find in its roar
The answers that will not come.

He speaks to me
In the early sound of the morning
And in the dim light of the evening
I can feel him in the day rising
I see him in the glint of your eye
I hear him in the innocence
Of children playing.
I see him all the time
He is in everything
He is everywhere
It's only a matter of opening
The eyes.
The roar of the sea
Is shouting answers out to me.

B B B
For Brendan Brophy

His arms were flying about
In all directions
As if he were trying to kill
A bee
He had things to say alright
And would say it
To whoever took the time to
Listen.
At unexpected times
There was a pleasure
In his eyes.
When someone might
have the good manners
To be a real man,
look at him and see
God
In him.
Arms flying
Funny to look at
Always killing bees.

O Riada Mass
for Fr Jim

It is as if
They are calling
In their calling
Waiting
In this waiting
Hoping for a beginning.
Their singing
Rises slowly up
To the highest places
Far above over heads.
In the joy of this
Beginning
We are childlike
In our hearts again
Through the language
Of my own true people
Sailing out of the sea
The sweet smell of incense
From the smoke,
The heat and fire
In the heat and
In the turning
In the lust of all our making
It is the beginning.
Á Iosa, Á Iosa.
In the gathering of fish
In the depths of bread
In the somewhere of what happens
The curling
Shimmering of begetting
Everything is caught

In a moment of itself
How the small bend
In a single voice
Weaves itself
Into me, lost
Turning on the
Road for home.

For Harry

He collected all
Of his integrity up
And made it
Come to life
In an old wheelbarrow
Lovely colour here he said
Just a little something
To brighten up
The back garden.

Memories of Charleville
For Connie Vance

Here he is a forty year old child
Awe struck in the autumn of the trees
It has always been so
Under his feet,
They fold into each other
Soft and pleasant
And wet in the sun
It is teasing his eye
With freckles of gold
The light almost frightens him
Tall and so old in their shade
But he is so small and young
And begins to count his
Time in footsteps
His days in the length
It takes a leaf
To fly into the past
And to know that nothing
Lasts forever
Except what has always been
And can sometimes be seen
Under trees
Slowly undressing themselves
In the wind.
A child on a wild morning
Of discovery
Is reborn again.

Let the hair sit
for Healy

If I could make you one
In plain white
No frills just simple
I would make it just for you
A wimple for your head.
You are gentle
Now that I think
About you
Looking busy in the quiet street.
This light
This orange artificial light
Is not for you;
You should be on soft grass
Under trees
Their shade to shadow you.
This is the place
I wish for you;
Soon to be in grief you say.
We all live our lives in grief
Living only for a moment.
Like
The speed of a hare
Going over long grass
Or to hear the breath of her
Sighing in the early morning
When rain makes the running hard
And the sky as near as yesterday
I would curl my locks
If I were you
Toss my head into the nearest breeze

Be content
With whatever I found.
Grab onto every day
Try never to grow old
Throw back whatever curls
I had left
And laugh into
The broad sky.

An Egg for Ken at Breakfast
For Ken McElroy

Your soft little yellow eye
The one I saw last night
When I lay down to dream a while
Before you died of fright
You cracked and into blubbery
Splash you swam
Round and round
In there you ran
But couldn't escape
The morning pan
Now before me here you sit
You know I'm going to enjoy
Eating you
Bit by every little bit.

Final

What wisdom you discern
In the dark
Of your thoughts
Utter in ordinary words
In the daylight.

Pussy Pissy Bed
(Leabáidh Múin Cait)

O pussy
My poor pussy
How I love you
Soft in my hand
Warm all over me
Purring me to sleep.
But you little bitch
You made my bed a ditch
But I still love you very much
I forgave at first
The wine had helped my thirst
but you
Left water in my nest.
My poor pussy
That was just the limit girl
So
You made me sleep
Out on my own
And as I head to town
I think of you and frown
But
You being pussy
I can't help but forgive
And say that
I still love you.

The most lonely sound in the quiet
Of the countryside must be the faraway sound of
a chainsaw.

Trees
For Tom Prior

Will you stop and see
A tree
Will you learn
From how it grows
Slow but sure strong and true
Graceful in the early and the evening light

Do you know the life it gives
To insects in their quiet ways
A home for birds to rest and live
The busy bee and the bumble bee
All God's creatures love the tree.

Across the sky they bow their heads
And wave their arms
A high breeze making tunes
To move the heart
The songs they sing
To me the humble poet
Trying to write their words
Will you listen
Will you see what I
Can sometimes see
All the mystery of these living trees.

After Work

After work

That comfort you might feel
When the day's work is over
You put your jacket on
Look for just a minute
At what got done
This is a special type of content
Your coat hugging you again
Like a balm
On the day's furious rush
You go home
Hopefully it all starts again
Early
In the morning.

Away from home
for Liz

I have my own life
Far away
From family and home
Nothing is ever familiar
I am constantly in the
Strange place of myself.
In the laughter of my face
I think of you and home
Something simple like,
Weeding the garden,
You are in my head
In the morning
My thoughts are always; of you
In the shed looking
For a fork
Or a spade you left
Where now its not.
I am far away from home
Lost in the unfamiliar
But I am thinking
Of you.

The Spirit

Illuminated by the sun
At mid day
I am looking at the bubble
Of my spirit level
I watch for the plumb line
To settle.
My spirit is now in
Perfect balance
In the heat and light
Of this day.

A Knock at the Door

People came to the house
To look for money
I knew by the knock
A definite give me knock
Not a
Hello it's nice to see you knock
Standing with the sun
At their backs
Staring into your bones
Into the next room
To try to find your guilt
They don't believe you
When you say
You don't have any
As soon as you have
Do let us know
And we will come
To give you pardon.

Old Houses

For Scallion

Finding the old house
Caught between
Its destination.
Coming from another time;
Someday our work will
Be deciphered and explained away
To some child not yet born
Sauntering up a gravelway
To take notes of photographs.
When our hammer sounds
Will be
Lost among the nettles.

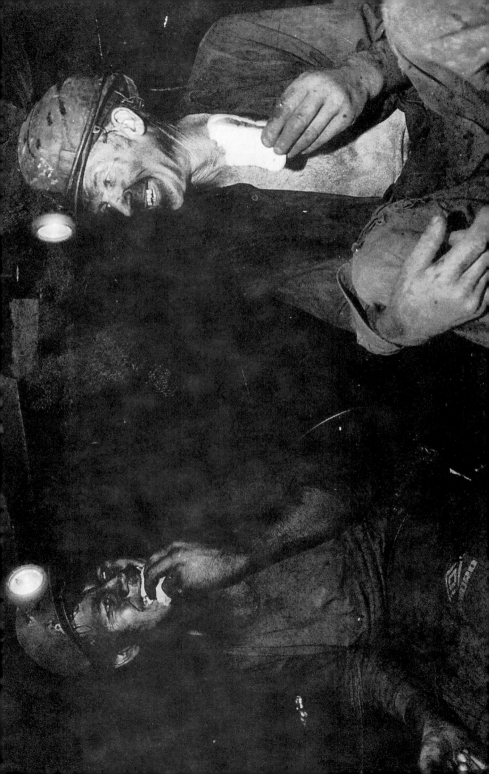

Living

Eventually we all lived our lives
On the edge of things
We died young and were
Forever estranged with the people
That we really loved
Money was never an issue
Because of the fear that it
Brought with it
We never understood
What qualities it ever had.
Stone wall mad we were;
Or so some called us
Holding their position
With their imaginary status
Established out of some inheritance.
Yes
We all died young and forgotten
Flowing into the world
Quietly
In the occasional rain shower
And sometimes whispering
Our words,
Softly
In the sounds of birds
Or in the wind
High up; in the trees
Where the leaves sometimes sigh.
Living
Just on the edge of things.

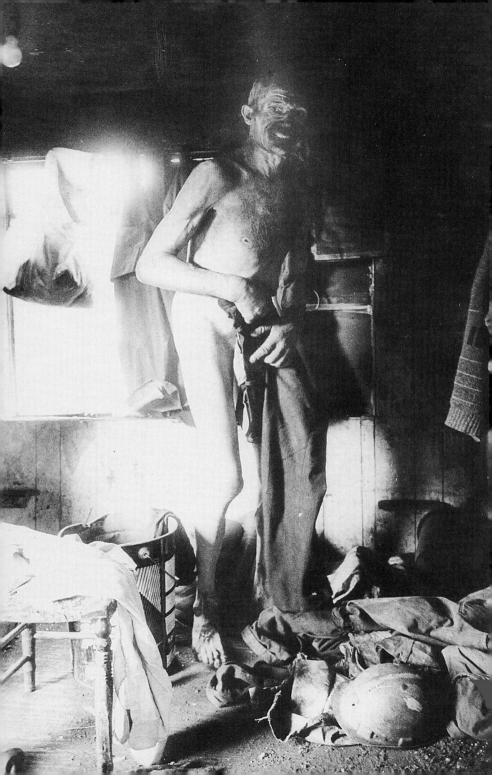

Look at him

No one could understand
His grief
Drunk on payday
Always on payday
Holding onto the counter
With both hands
He is gentle in his loneliness
Weak with all the noise
Of laughter
This room so full of laughable sin

Other people
On their way to somewhere
And he just about able
To negotiate the door
Out into the night neon
Both hands safe in his pocket
Not quite empty yet
Still a jingle left
To take him to his nowhere room

The morning sun
Brought the day into sharp focus
Real with the noise of early traffic
The sound of the boom
Going into first gear

He got up out of bed
To look for his integrity.

The Ranger
For P.G.

He was much older now
And quiet in the noise
Of the crowd
His quietness seemed to shout
Inside him
His voice more measured, almost gentle
Age had made his eyes deep
The wildness of his younger days
Was hidden here
He was going back and into time
Dancing on a kitchen floor
Grabbing her around her waist
Singing at the top of his voice
The fiddles and accordion music
Filled his thoughts
Then he reached for his pint
And drank down today.
His long road to here
Had quiet sunny places still
That he could travel back to
Riding his strong black bike
Under the high leaves
Past the elder ditches
Hanging heavy with blackberries
Strung out in the long grasses
The smell of nettles
In the early light
Rushing off to work
He took another swallow of his pint
Down past the half way mark
Drinking deep in the dark
The bitter taste of today on his lips.

Freckle Pus
For Margaret

Freckle Pus
Ya fast thing ya
You broke out of
The trap in jig time
Stay on track
Like a Greyhound Bus
My freckle pus
Tear on yer best
Sandy girl your hair
Your tail, high
In the air.
Take all my cares
Away
Your high smile
Your golden wink
Saved me
Just when I
Began to sink

Good on ya
Freckle pus
Tear on yer best

The Lilting Light

There near the water sound
In the yellow of the grass
The quiet lilacs
Bow their purple heads
To the sea.

A thin thread of wire
Stretching out
From stake to stake
Their unevenness
Innocent and blameless
Just holding each other.

A lone sheep
High in the sky
Kneeling into the mean grass
Praying for forgiveness.

The rocks are content
To be themselves
In whatever shape
They happen to be.

All are lilting
The not knowing of what
The heat of the sun
In the ever changing light is doing
It decides for us
What it is it wishes
Us to see.

Painting April

It is April
Early
The sky meets the fields
Painted soft pink
Against the day rising

Today the men will come
To walk in the wide bog
Soon the first turf
Will be cut into rows

The dark brown scraggy sods
Squelching sound and squeezed out
Then the rich dark, the best turf
Like a definite pencil line

Drawn out ready for the soft colours
Diluted out in rain
Softly blown in wind
Moulded hard and strong in warm sun

All the once tall oaks
Are buried there
Held fast in the deep soft belly
Alone not belonging to any tree
Or itself reborn from acorns

Today in April men will come
To measure out the new turf
The early morning is painted pink
In the brown dark bog.

Just another hill walk
For Derek

Have you ever walked
In the rain
Totally naked
Without even socks or boots on
Drops belting down onto
All the delicate parts
Both nipples erect
The eyes half closed
The hair as if
Someone had stuck it
With gum.
And the thin breeze, biting you.
The freedom of it
The total madness of it
Imagine the laugh you could have
Telling your friends.
They look at you with
Their ears open
Their eyes bright
And you sitting there
Explaining how airtight
Every body, any body becomes
When theirs is under pressure
Even the girls are laughing
With the imagination truly aroused
Nervous
At the sight of you with nothing but
Your socks and boots on.

Red Wine

Let me stay forever
In your high company

Let us sometimes get
Warm with words

Forgetting the world; and work
Let us leave trouble behind for a while

Let us look into each other's hearts
And allow each other the privilege of a
smile.

Tractor Story
Ballaghmore Castle

For Grainne Ní Cormack

At first I thought
This is great.
Herself goes off, and gets me two new
wheels.
You should have seen me
Ready to go to town I was
In my new shoes.
I was really looking forward to it.
Then they parked me
Parked me, if you don't mind,
At the back of the shed.
You have no idea
How it feels to get parked.
Anyway,
I stayed silent, and have to
Admit went all into myself.
Well you would too if you were
Ignored for almost two years
Only I'm a tractor I would have
Cried tears.
People came and went
Without even a nod in my direction.
Even at Christmas, nothing happened
Not even a child playing pretend
Ploughing.
Then all of a sudden in October
Herself
And some tall bearded fella
With a hat
Switches my thoughts on

My spout full of all last
Year's rain
And the pain it gave me
She starts spraying hot air
Into my private passage
God was I embarrassed
I tried my living best
To start
But my chest was full of water
I spat out black water
All over herself.
Serves her right for ignoring me
And parking me in the first place.
Then out of somewhere
The excitement of it all just got to me
I even lifted my transport box
Every piston plunged power throughout me
All of a sudden I pulled away
From the briars and the nettles
speeding down towards the main road.
O the pure thrill of it
All up and down the avenue we went.
All day I worked
Going backwards and forward
It was one of those days
I wished would last forever.
So here I am parked up
Only for the night mind
Dreaming of a busy winter
Or part-time work
I mean even once a week

Would do.
Rumour has it that they're getting
Me a new coat for Christmas
Blue on top, and my favourite red.
So what do you think of that?
One minute all lonely inside myself
But now, alive again
Puffing smoke into the sky
Over Ballaghmore Castle
In my new shoes, my red and blue
Coat, Ready to go to town.
If you see me give me a wave
Or better still come to the
Castle for a visit.
Herself will be delighted.

Serving his time

He was hitching a lift earlier that day
I caught a glimpse of his eyes
Only just
Only just in the dark
And here he is with that smell of timber
On his sleeves
Sawdust still on his shoulders
His eyelids are falling into his pint
The floor is a faraway place
Near his feet
Standing there determined not to go
Home till closing time
Because then morning will be a certainty
And he will pull the morning onto his feet
The best of the worst socks
Near his clothes
Hanging on the floor
But then today is Sunday
So he will walk out and down
In his Sunday best
Early Mass a prayer to the ceiling
Into the pub to the cosy warm of the crowd
I was him once; I did what he does
But then I caught the glimpse
Of someone elses eye.

After All

Silence 8 x 3

It is the light bending red or yellow
That you see in the quiet dust
Rising out of coloured glass.

The heavy weight
Of yourself outside yourself
Lying awake in the dark.

It is the grass
Just being itself
Bending in early drops of water.

When the lawnmower stops
Then you get lost
In the quiet smell of new grass.

When you lie on the
Flat of your back
Just you and the sky.

When the children have stopped
Playing
And the street lights come on.

When you put your coat
On after work
Then wait for a minute.

When the cat climbs
up on your lap
And purrs you to sleep.

For Emma White

Her blue eyes
In the morning
Shine from the
Gold in her hair

She is calling
To the child in me
From out of everywhere
It is in
Her thoughts
I wish for her to find me

In my hands
I will forever fold her
And in this holding
Teach her how
The love she gives
As only Emma could.
Is higher than the
Highest apples
In the apple wood

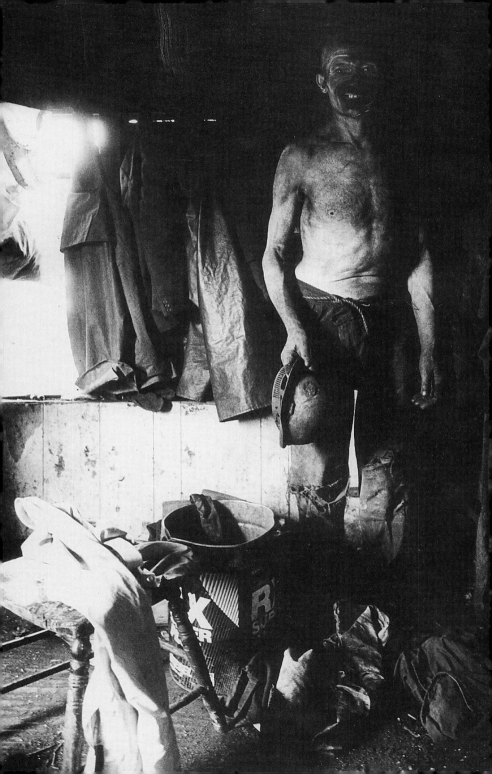

Some Angels

For Dudley and Bonnie

I have met with many angels
Most of the ones I've met wore caps
But they don't all wear caps
The odd one may even be bald.

Some of them nowadays
Even drive cars
It's hard to tell them apart
From other people.

Sometimes you will see a glint
In their eyes
Watch out for it
When soft rain has fallen
And there's a rainbow in the sky.

They may not even smile at you
The best ones will often
Frown at you
But when they do smile
Good things are about to happen.

And the hair might stand
Up on the back of your neck
A lot of angels have arthritis
And use walking sticks
Just so they can blend in
Some are even young
With lots of freckles.

You don't have to go out of your way
To find them
They may have found you already
And are doing their best to keep you
In the palm of their hand.

Rachel

Like all children
How they look at you
After mischief
The blue of
Your Christmas eyes
Are bright in the
Cold frost of winter
You make me merry
With joy
Watching you.
You are the holly
In the green of snow
Rachel
My red berry.
You know already
How Christmas rings
That bell.
And calls me back
To tell you
How I love you.

Spring is coming

The houses are slowly
Revealing themselves
Pushing their shapes up into the light
A gable end; a chimney; a television aerial
A signal to the world
All the white of the frost
Still asleep on the slated roof
Weeping into the gutters
Flowing back to where the birds have been
Even they are busy flying, little silhouettes
Leapdancing through the broad sky.
Out over the trees
That have waited all winter
They are never tired
Holding their arms up alive again
They know that spring is coming.

Whiskey Still
For William Broderick

Make a soft and tender touch
Make your fingers join with mine.
Hold on to me
Close and close.
And closer still
A moment quiet now after rain.
With just the sound
Of drip and drop.
Cold stars wink and shine
And stop me
Thinking of the past too much.
Across the fields
The weather changes.
Makes the dark bird's journey out
To travel off into the morning.
A soft and mossy August day.
The grass is shining
Green and yellow.
Glows into my eyes.
I hear the Kilworth bell ring out
A good day coming surely.
Not much risk of rain today
A day to cut the barley.
Cut down into barley straw.
And left to lie like rows of fluffy paper.
Pile in the grain hard rich and ripe.
Taken from the fields to
Still ferment and sour
To sweet and bitter whiskey.
Yes hold me close then closer still.

A Dream of Flight
For Dennis

In my young time
All I see before me
Belongs to me and us
No need for forgiveness yet
For days not yet lived out
Soon my dreams will soar
Into the air in flight
Gliding over wind and rain
Away into the sun

Moving
Like a small lonesome bird
Leap flying
Through a damp morning
Softly
It's wings against the dark air
Gliding down to almost touch
The far ground
Going from its pillow time
With little moving sounds

Across where there once were meadows
Knowing that it was there
Long shadows rolled across
The fields below the sun
Sometimes resting quiet among
The few leaves left
Before they fall
Into the new autumn
Of the year.

Now that I am old
And all my dreams have flown
I still have little dreams
Ready in their nest
In all my toiling rain and wind
I look into the sun
Believing
That to live well
Is to always dream

Like a small lonesome bird
Leap flying
Through the air
I move on
I remember a dream of flight
In a damp September morning.

Croghan Farmer
For John and Nicola

He was just standing there
Startled at the sound of our car
Cornering the road
The wet grasses licking
The sides of his boots
He looked as if he was studying
His cattle his future
Planning ahead
Watching their form in the half light
Even now I realise
I will always remember him
Surprised by the sound of a passing car
He has I suppose forgotten
Us already
And you reading are painting
Pictures in your head
Of a farmer in Croghan
A long time ago
Startled by light
Watching his future in the form
Of his cattle.

Dancing in the Apple Wood
For Tansy Cowley

Even if they hear a wheeze
They vanish quicker than a sneeze
Out late singing high go ding
High jinks in the apple wood in June

I saw them once the fairy men
Dancing in the rhyming light
In between the windfalls in the wood
Their fiddles bright, their music sweet
All through the night the magic beat
Swinging with the last light of the moon

If you go there out to the trees
Keep down low or on your knees
They don't like strangers coming near
Keep very quiet in case they hear.

You could end up singing high go ding
Dancing high jinks
Skipping with the fairy men
In between the windfalls
Altogether; in the apple wood.

Red Shirt Day
For Mick O'Toole

It was a blue sky
Wind swept
Rain coming out of nowhere
Delgany day.

I could see a red shirt wave to me
From half a mile away

Was it calling me before the rain
Or telling me to stay
Bending in a Monday breeze
the wind decides our fate

I walked across to look
Under a slow gathering of rain
A silent filling in of squally grey
Brings the heavy tipping sounds
Tumbling to the waiting grasses
Into craving clay.

A red shirt sleeve waves to me
In a wind swept
Rain coming out of nowhere
Delgany day
Underneath the blue sky
The wind decides our fate.

Cutting Timber
For Seani Byrne

You are three hundred years old
With that tiny seed there in your hand
I saw you dropping it through the fog
I was lucky to see you
Child of my past
Tall person of my future
We are underneath trees
All standing ready to greet the turn of leaves
Quiet in themselves Moving
In the peculiar blush of a single breeze.
Now we are wise and so suddenly old.
Some are content
Others looking back making their day
constant
Or perhaps in torment for a word said
A word long gone back into water
Or words tumbling over stones
Out into the sea.
Words trampled underfoot into soft ground
Curled up with hooves of cattle or sheep
Growing up through grasses
Driving the roots of trees
Making tall broad leaves and branches
Mysterious in their shaking
Concealed inside the bark
Counting time in rings
For the cutter to reveal when felling
And we open time with sawing
We see something no one else has ever seen
There it is deep in wood

Words from out of the past
And we are privileged to be here to see it
And to listen - wise at last and so suddenly
old.

After Life

Leather Straps

For Jack Brennan and Tommy Smullen

He was content to be himself
With black wax
Making thread for sewing
Through his pipe smoke
There was leather
Ready for the making
Straps and loops
Collars and winkers
For men to attend to horses
Straddles and bellybands.

And men making music
The accordion soothing pain
Wherever it went
Those straps held together
With handmade thread
As good today
As they were meant to be

And we too should be content
To still see thread
Holding straps for a simple accordion
Because there is music
Ready for the listening.

Whenever

For Fr Declan, John's Lane Church, Dublin R.I.P.

He learned his Latin well
In grey morning fog
The chanting.
His voice rose above the spires
To the sky.
He found the secrets of himself
In other people;
The genuflection's in his knees
His hands in the cold
Stone of the water.
It's rippling out
The chiselling in
The shape of past;
The light, the dark.
This trembling in the water sound
The flick of drops across the air
The fingers touching;
Forehead
A murmur soft, the chalice glints
The blood; the breaking bread.
You becoming one
Then the sound
You hear manoeuvring, drawing
In the air
A drone of pipes
Like a drift of bees
Calling out of space
And you saw the
Face of God appear
You felt his hands close by.

His warm embrace
Will soothe your tears.
And just think of it
Just two of you go walking.
In some wood
The sun will draw your shadows
Over fields
We will see you, soft below the clouds
Wishing for the grace of words
To bring you near.
And we will see heaven;
Whatever that is
Whenever we can.

Rain Falling – The Curragh 2000

For Fr O'Byrne

In the curious and the early light
There is something about
The way we look at things
The faraway with
Our imaginary eye
Turning the colours into strange shapes
Against the sky.
In soft rain
I dip my fingers
Into its cold memory
Touch it onto my forehead
I bring this clay of my people
Into the present light
Knowing that I will become someday
The dust under my children's feet
Rain falling into folds
Will one day let me
Touch their faces
In the curious and the early light.

For Alex Hughes
Poet and Doctor
To Vera

Let me rest in a little;
Peace only.
Come any time
And disturb me.
Wrapped in cold clay
Sit near and whisper
Poems to me
Or hum a tune
into the air,
Let wild flowers be
my eiderdown.
With simply country birds
In flight
To chirp and keep me
Company there.

Eating Sausages

She said
They assembled
His teeth carefully
Even though his face
Was dead.

She remembers the day well
He went on his first trip
To the dentist

How good he looked
Coming through the hall door
With the boots he promised
He would buy her
Whenever or
The next time he was
In town.

Then she did
What was expected
Dropped
The flowers she picked for him, all of them
Down through the air to land
On top of him
Had a sigh
Ambled off to the pub
With the crowd

To drink; sing a few songs
And eat cocktail sausages.

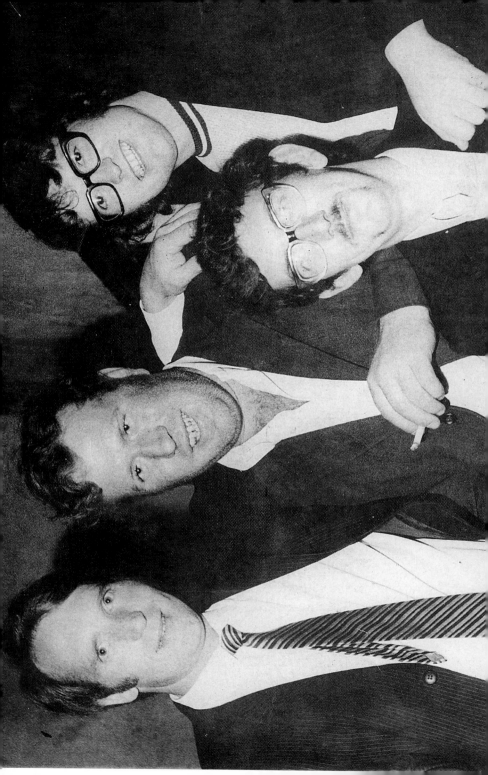

Photo 1971

All smiling and happy
Looking out to the future
Four wild Irish men
High as kites and on the skite
From work; no doubt
Celebrating
Sam Maguire's final arrival
Andy smiling into the night saying
"I'll tell ya one thing"
Big Nick laughing as usual
After a hard day's work
Finbar with his mad stripy tie
Loving everyone
Prionnsias with his Frank Zappa look
Merry all throughout.
That was September 1971
Willie Brien, McTiege
McCormack and Kilmurray
With their brave Offaly team
Sent all our worries astray
High into the wind
That was then; this is now
How things happen in between
And the way time flies
Brings tears sometimes to the eyes
Me sitting looking at the past
Four wild young Irishmen
Smile back to me in the future.

Dancing

It was like a jig
The way the ground danced
The fog just resting on Croghan Hill
All the green coming alive
Through the white frost
This is what it is to live
To see all this
And realise
How small you have to become
I sit saddleways on a roof
Looking as often as the work allows
The frost eating at my hands.

Summer in Ypres
For Francis Ledwidge

In Serbia you walked
Beneath the dark sky of war
When your thoughts cried
For a childhood place

Green near the Boyne
A far golden time
A ticking cottage clock
when childhood rhymes caressed you

Remember; you knew at the bridge
When blackbirds flew
In the mystery of clouds
In streams of reeds below your feet

Little did you dream
Your folding time
Would not see thirty summers
But you are born again

In wind and rain
Drops chasing drops
Falling every falling, this
Softens the pain of losing you

To a field of white standing stones.

Celebrating life with a well laid table
A hand stitched duck and glasses of fine red wine

The Wren's Farewell
for Michael Hartnett

You and I would go walking
Up to the Northbrook Hotel
Nice and slow with your cap
Secure
Waving your stick
Slow and casual
We'd wander for a pint and a short
Time later you introduce me to your friends
A poet
You gave me a swelled head that day.

On all souls night we ate duck
With that special stitching in her bum
Barm brack and red wine
Then we all flew around the room
On imaginary broomsticks
Laughing at the madness of it
Then falling into the couch
Like bould children.

Then you go away to a quiet room
Yourself and your thoughts
Listening to Finlandia;
Sibelius breaking the silence.
A little wren waking up at all hours
Standing there conducting;
Conscious of C sharp minor
You were the poet all right

Struggling with some roman scribe
Sitting, writing in his sandals.

Since your going
I have tended not to look at things
Walls are stone in the face
Trees a shape to the sky
And the leaves always the leaves
Constantly changing the light.
In the early stem of frost
In its tumbling and its folding out
I look for words to say;
Written underneath my feet
In the secret language of small birds.
Their letters printed into clay.
With their feet
They make the words for going away.
I am reading in the quiet where
There is forever a trace of you.

But there are no words for me to speak
Just the sounds of small birds
Their coming and their leaving
I wait for the listening
Of a wren's farewell.

Michael
You left us with the words;
That's all we need to say.

The Artist Sleeps
for Robert Lenkiewicz, Plymouth

And then it happened
Right in the middle
Of an ordinary day
His white flowing hair
No longer had its warmth
From out his head and deep inside
His heart it came
The love he loved
The care he gave
To Plymouth.

The sculptured wood
The brazen brush across
A canvas
At peace with the paint
Understanding the colours

Strolling out into the light
His heart stopped
Its rhythm
In the music of the day
In the sounds of the street
He sleeps
In the city.

Maudlin Road
for Eugene

He looked the part at first
When I met him
Like a hard man
Stout heavy set with
The hands of a man
That grafted hard
Tough looking too
With that boxer's nose.
But then I got to see
His gentle ways
His gardening fingers
That quiet pride he had in
The middle of cabbages
And potatoe stalks – or lost
In the colours of flowers
Blooming at his shoulder
A Kerry man in Kells
And she small and neat
Busy at crosswords
As broadminded as the wind
Looking over her glasses at you
As proud as punch of herself
Wrapped up in her fur coat
Full of fun and elegant about town
Now both gone into some other room
Waltzing in each others arms
Or just gone off to the races
John and Mayphie laughter glowing
In their faces.

Back to the shop
for Margaret

The sun is calling
Its light over all the ground
In its usual way
Changes do not bother the sun
Tullacanna is today
Like every other day
Busy being itself.
It might be Monday
Wet in Wexford
Pints
And more with them
Fill the air with conversation
There will be talk of
Dogs and Horses
The odds on – the favourite
The time spent wondering.
And there I see his girls
Delighted on nostalgia day ˙
In their pony and trap
Everyone goes back to the shop
The sun is
Also throwing its warm light
Over Kilcaven
And somedays even
In the half light
Of rain
You can almost
Imagine Heaven.

The grasses cross
Themselves into
The light
From Ballymitty
To Tullacanna
Bending their heads
For Mick Stafford
Who calls me
Sometimes out of
Memory
Back to the shop.

Where Peace Begins
for Michael in Cree

The heart shakes
Like a wound in timber
All those established men
With their collars worn
Out from reading
How they compose themselves
On the altar.
Your mother waiting
For you in the cold.

All your tears lie
At the back of your next breath
Men are busy deep in clay
On this day you will
Consecrate the ground
Beneath the roots of trees
And stones in their peculiar
Resting place
You have found the space
Where the heart shakes
And where peace begins.

With her thoughts

For Freda

She was fine
And the way she looked
At me
Or touched me
Sometimes with
Her thoughts
That turn of her head
Her smile turning the room
Her hands on her hips
And those lips talking
I would stand under a tree
With her.
I would look across a bog with her
She could see things
Hidden in the landscape
Invisible but always there
How fine she was
And the way a stone wall
Weary in its waiting
Stood for us. Just
Children walking through time
She with birds on her mind
Ditches stretching off
Into her imagination,
A turn in the road
A field with a hill or hollow;
She would walk
And I would follow
Waiting for the sounds of small birds

In their nesting.

In my dreaming
I have cried out for her
And sometimes
I cry for her with tears in my sleep.
Somedays now
I saunter down
By the canal
To look across
At contented horses
In a field where there are trees;
And where they and the horses
See themselves
Looking back at each other
In the green of the water
She is still
Touching me,
Sometimes with her thoughts.

Near Ellen's
for Declan Conway

Everything has its opposite
Night pulls itself like a sock
Over the day.
You are forever travelling along
A sun filled sky
Over the fields near Ellen's.
You are going to a place
Where there are no margins;
No length of time.
Without even a circle to navigate.
As for us, we do not know for sure
If such a place exists.
But you exist somewhere near
In the landscape of our memory
In the flying away of a bird
In the sound of the sea
In the song of a fish
In the shape of things
Where were you going at all.
Last night's moon
Still red in your memory
Something beckoned your eye
A bird, a hare calling you
Headlong towards them.
The road ticked away into
The heat of the sun
Suddenly you are forever fourteen.

At times the shape of the landscape
    The flying sounds of a song
    Things like birds with a memory of fish;
    Of being lost at sea and we like the world
    Are left
To live in sudden times.

Funeral Home

The hands are white
Without movement
Of any kind
Woven into each other
At the fingers.

Looking perfect in the light
The face as solid as stone
The lips touch the air
Without a tune to whistle
Everything suddenly frightens me
He does not hear the rain
It is cold
The mouth is dry without spittle
Something heavy pulls
At the shoulder.

The curls of his hair are
Twisted into willow
There is no dance left in his feet
The head is dull
Heavy on his
White pillow.

I find him woven into my past
Forever light blue
At the fingers.

In the fields of Yalu
From The Book of the Dead

In the beautiful west
Are the fields of Yalu
Where the sun sets.
From the east we begin
To fly to the sun
Born there to journey here.
I saw men quiet with tears
in their eyes.
In the land of fairy mist
To rest for a short time
In the fields of Yalu.
Looking back into smoke and mist
Hear music in the wind.
Tambourines from a distance
Beating out into a dance.
The cliff vibrates all in a trance
Finding bliss in the beautiful west
Across the fields of Yalu.
We will rise again into a breeze
Like dust and leaves
Left by the wind that comes from the west.
Out from the fields of Yalu.
In the East we began
To fly to the Sun
Here time has no age
At last to rest at our journeys end
Together forever
In the fields of Yalu.

For a girl in Kilmihil
For Geraldine H

Someday I will die
And be among the flowers and the bushes
I will be the fragrance that
Awakens you
Walking somewhere
Along your road to home
You may be young
Carrying your memories with you
Into the far distance.
But we are always here;
Forever outliving ourselves
Confused everyday
With the simple words of men
Passing each other on the busy street
Without time to speak.
Every minute we die a little
Mellowing out into a new shape
A leaf perhaps
Tumbling into quiet grass
Silent in the flowers
Safe at last among the bushes
Falling and changing shape
A simple fragrance
In the air.

Cuimhneacháin ar mAthair

*(Measuring) – Version my Mary Troy &
Cathal Ó Searcaigh*

Buaileas leo siúd im óige
An gluín úd sin
A thomhasfadh is a ghearrfadh
An tadhmad úd lena rialóir fillte
Orlaigh, troigh is slat
Sna laetha sin in óige m'athair.
Bhraitheas é, uair,
Nuair a bhíos a cúig
Ag dearadh fuinneog do thig Danny Hanlon
Fuaim an sabh i gciúnas an trathnóna
An plána ag sleamhnú is ag siosadh
Thall is anall ag caitheamh
Píosaí adhmaid ina loch oír
Timpeall a bhróig
Thógas iad i mo lámha beoga páistiúla
Boladh úr mhilis an adhmaid sa srón.
Thug m'athair aoibh dom
Is rinne folt den chrus
A thit siar thar mo chluasa.
In aois a cúig, lig m'athair dom
É a fhaire ag saothrú go dian
Cúig bliana eile, bhíos a deich
Is m'athair sínte romham - marbh.
Ag tochailt na huaighe
Bhriseadar an fód is gearradh an chré
Le láí, lá Lúnasa.
Thomhas siad a fhaid is a mhéid
Bhí a shean-rialóir adhmaid
Greamaithe go daingean i mo láimh
Is chuireas sa chré é
Mar piliúr faoina cheann.

Two Mile House

You died in the early morning
The whole day ahead of you,
In your nurses uniform
You worked all night.
All I could do
Was to hold your hand,
Close your eyes
Your sight was gone.
I whispered the Our Father
For you into your ear.
People standing there said she's dead.
Then the firemen came.
I never cried for you
Just whispered prayers for you,
A young Kilkenny nurse
Killed in the early curse
Of a frosty Monday morning.

.

Therese

Time is forever time
Moments are just places
Where we have
Always been
Sometimes in a brief
Moment of beginning
We forever remember
Each other
My brothers and my father
And my mother
Longing for another
Brought me here
In their longing
I found out the light
And know that I will
In their long memory
Be Therese
I will be the constant
Of their constant light
Forever
Just a moment
In the places
And in their faces
I will always be.

Lost at Sea

For those lost in Fethard-on-Sea

Craoi-óg
I am at north
By north east
Variable
My thoughts
Are racing through
My young heart
Constantly thinking
Of the south.

I am all at sea
Again
I know where tears begin
They are falling
Out of time and rhyme
Into a stone
Near my shoulder.

This stone is where
My heart should be
With the things
I can't forget.

Lost somewhere
Far away
North by north east
My thoughts
Are towards
The south.

For Fr Andrew Mullen
Buried in Killaderry aged 28 in 1818

With things sufficient
For my needs
I am sitting
A walking stock
To hit nettles
My cap to save heat
A cigarette sending out
Signals that I am here
Imagining your warm hands
In a still place
It is not dark there
You show us even now
With signposts
To direct our steps
We are trying to find our road
To your perfect light
Underneath the sun
Our lands are fast asleep
There is quietness here
And sometimes
We are lost here
Along a narrow road
Looking for compassion
We offer to you
Those things
We cannot
Put into words.

The River

He looked so well
The sun was at his shoulder.
His future lay behind him
In the bustle and the noise.
this must be it
This must be where his
Past had been hiding all along.

In the slow soothing reach
Of the river.

All he had to do was touch it
Feel it
Put his hands out
Go on be a man,
This felt right, this at last
Was where his redemption hid.

He felt so overwhelmed
Soon he would feel all that love
All those people
Who never understood him
His past enveloped him.
It felt cold at first.

But soon the pressure reassured him
Pressing in on him
Like never before
The drunken hazy evening
Was his insulation
His isolation
His statement to the world.

He knew deep down
It was his family,
The love that was there
The love he had every waking minute
For them.
That's what kept him going.
He knew the ones he loved
And cared about so much
Would never understand him
He thought about his sins
This was the excuse for going off the tracks.

The drunkeness kept him safe
He could feel it
That strong embrace of forgiveness,
That welcoming
That river smell
That warm soothing touch.

The last thing he saw
Was a small bird
Carrying a stick,
He was floating down the river
Into his future.

Next day they said
Foul play was not suspected.

Letter from ESTA
for Jerri

Because I was your beginning,
I mean I was there are the start
The words never came to me
When I was with you.
Just as part of my journey
With you is ended
You and I are at our beginnings,
I am in a new transient light
It is so bright here
There is no doubt here
Or anger or even fear of anything
I wish you could see it
How utterly tangible and real
The love is.
So now to let you know
That I have only left the room for a while
Going on ahead so to speak
I want you to know
That we are not yet parted.
This is not an end
It just seems that way
I think I am allowed to be sometimes
Near your shoulder
Give me a few days
So that I can have my hat at the ready
I think all you need to do
Is need me to call.
That I may become real again
And not be forever away
That I am a picture to you, coming from the
negative.
Shalom Alachem.

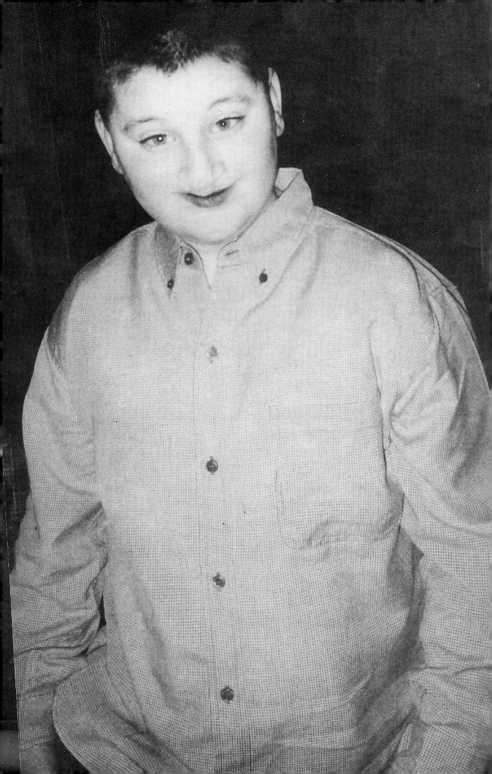

For Damien

I see him
He is running
Laughing
Underneath the broad stretch
Of the chestnut tree.

His laughter
Is the rustle
I hear coming through
The leaves.

We still call our
Children
To come home from their play
But your father called you
Home so young
It took our breath away.

So we carried you and
Smiled for you
We tumbled and we
Folded you in flowers
To let their petals
Tuck you in.

Will you now be the
White May blossom
Growing in this rowan tree
I know there will be
Days again when you will run
And hurry back to me.

Birr

For Peter Hynes

Rirb is a word that is total nonsense
Irbr is no better
Ribr sounds even worse
To the sounds of the sweet lap of the
Camcor
The Birr of the water
Calls out in the evening

The sun in its usual way cannot stay longer
Across the rooftops and steeples
There is an echo of horses
Soldiers marching away
Military men content in barracks
Crinklening into sleep
Poor old Cumberland with his only foot
remaining
Has his big tow pointing down Main Street
To the boys of Manchester

There is a high elegance
To the streets and the squares
The heavy rock or classic sounds in
Oxmantown Hall

All is calling you in

The moon and the stars overhead are
familiar
With its giant eye to heaven;
In the trees and high scent of the castle
garden

My poor gardener no longer here
Just out of sight behind some weeding

And the people, the high and the low
Will tell you so
The pleasure and the love they have
Watch them alive to the Birr of the water

Forever home

The Noise of Men
For Francis Ledwidge

I am rich with what I see before me
Knowing there is always a surprise
In store
I wait again for the sun to rise
Bright before and light behind
I have chosen to be here
In the speeding past of the clock
Watching the city.

From underneath tall grass he comes
In his own time
Invisible to the eyes
Of mortal men
He sleeps at Boesinghe
Where bees are charging
From flower to ditch.
Asleep like pale woodbines
Or leaning against the dapple grasses
Golden at the stem for hay
In his death the living flowers
Reach up and out
A slow sigh
In their own time
And me...
I have chosen to be money poor
Among the speeding past of the city
The noise of men
The comfort that they seek
Will see me sitting just to watch
Looking at the inside of the city
I wait again for the sun to rise.

Obituary

The amount of time and energy
People spend on saying goodbye
We are at the beginning
Talking about the remains
And what remains of the day
Or the way they say things on the radio.
Names of the dead
Named for the living
Time of departure
Leaving at
Arriving at
Then in between the fertiliser ads
The mortgage rate
The latest hits
Sun spot destinations
Destiny itself carried
Into our listening room
The slowly living room
Extra strong coffee waking into Monday
He thought about a moonlight night
And about how sometimes
Arms surround you good and tight
He said
"Hello Mary Lou goodbye heart"
Everything was so utterly butterly
Everybody's busy saying goodbye
Someone's always leaving
Then it was news time.

A Tinker's Fire

For Val Hughes

Somedays I think
Who are tinkers anyway.
Those fine people
That carry the flame
And still have it.

Who are we
Bringing it indoors
First to shoot up the chimney
And now discreetly hidden
Underneath the stairs
With a low hum of energy.

O give me a tinker anyday
Above the words
And the swirl of talk
Looking at you with
That fire in the eye.

Forever carrying the flame
Into the everywhere
Of everyday.

Termon Angel

I am so tired
Leave me;
Let that brine
Drain out through
The pores of my skin
Eternally grateful
For this resting place
My heavy wings
My pale skin
My somewhat contemporary look
May seem strange at first
But do not be afraid
We glide to all sorts of places
I am visible
Only for a short while
Soon I will evaporate into
The deep ocean of beginnings
I am going forward
Forever caressing things.

Mojo Pin
for Jeff Buckley

Days will pass when we will not speak
There is forever lilac in my dreams of you
And there will be desolate nights below the
sky
The corpus christi of the air
There will be the constant light between us
The foxgloves where they hang their bells
Days will pass when we will not speak
If I could make it so I would turn their
petals into pulp
And there will be desolate nights below the
sky
I will ferment this colour into wine
There will be the constant light between us
But I must accept the grace by which you
speak
And there will be desolate nights below the
sky
You turn life over as a lover should
Days will pass when we will not speak
There will be a hallelujah in your coming
There will be the constant light between us
Your words go rising up into a carol in the
wind
And there will be desolate nights below the
sky
The water cold; your hair salty real, on my
tongue
Days will pass when we will not speak.

But there will be the constant light between us
And there will be desolate nights below the sky
But always the light
The constant light between us.

Cowboys and Indians
for the Brazil Family,
Catherine, David & Niamh

Here I am walking again
Into the unknown
Near the lazy yellow
Of the buachalan
The high garden is gone
The pink flowers hang down
Bowing in adoration
To the near distance
The sky is its usual grey
Heavy with rain

But there is a familiarity
For me, in the yellow
Of the lazy buchalans
Like a child running
Down a hill
Trampas at my side
On our imaginary horses
There are some days
Matty
That I think of you
And in my listening ear
Still miss you
Shooting me dead
In the Jar Mac's field
Shouting
You can't kill a running man
Then it's home to pulping turnips
Or going down the Green Lane for water
Tom Roes' cattle staring out

Waiting for us
Together on the ass and cart
Some days it's Friday
We're mitching from school
And we are going to the factory
For briquettes
Down by Henry Edgeils

I'm still here
Matty
Walking into the unknown.